CONTENTS

FROM EYE TO BRAIN

PHOTOGRAPHY DEPENDS ON LENSES AND A LIGHT-SENSITIVE MATERIAL TO FORM AND REGISTER AN IMAGE. HUMAN EYES WORK LIKE BIOLOGICAL CAMERAS AND THEY ARE A MARVEL OF DESIGN — COMPACT, AUTOMATIC, NEVER NEEDING BATTERIES OR FILM, AND USUALLY LASTING A LIFETIME.

We sense the world around us in five ways – touch, taste, smell, sight and hearing. Many people would say that sight is the most precious of the senses. The two, golf-ball-sized bags of jelly nestling in protective, bony hollows in our skulls, are remarkably complex and sensitive energy-converters. They change light into electricity. They respond to the rainbow spectrum of energy waves that floods our world by sending electrical signals racing to the brain. Inside the brain, this chaos of electricity is processed in ways that we are only just beginning to understand, to create the sensation of sight.

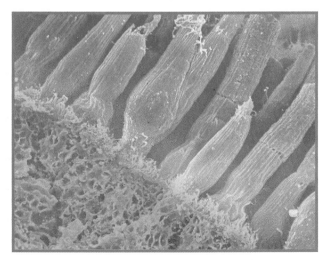

This false colour image of a retina is produced by a scanning electron microscope (see pages 14-15). It shows rods in blue and cones as green-blue.

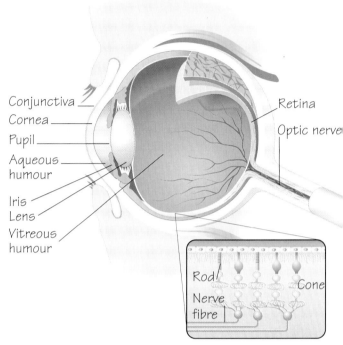

Light is focused on to the retina by a lens and changed into electrical nerve pulses by million of rods and cones in the retina.

THE BIOLOGICAL CAMERA

Light enters each eye through a transparent membrane, the cornea, which is protected by a transparent covering, the conjunctiva. The cornea bends the light and begins to focus it. The light travels on through a watery solution, called the aqueous humour, and through the pupil, a hole in the middle of the iris. The iris opens and closes automatically to control the amount of light entering the eye. Next, the light passes through the lens, which focuses a sharp image on the back of the eye. The light travels through the vitreous humour behind the lens and the focused image falls on to the retina, a layer of light-sensitive cells. The retina changes the image into electrical impulses which travel along the optic nerve to the brain.

That's the simple explanation, but what really happens is a lot more ingenious! There are two types of light-sensitive cells in the retina – rods and cones. Cones are sensitive to colour – some respond to red light, some to blue and some to green. Rods can't tell the difference between colours, but they are very good at detecting low levels of light. In bright light, cones give us colour vision. In dim light, rods take over.

The optic nerve cannot carry all of the visual information that the eye detects, so signals from sets of retina cells are combined before being sent to the brain. On the way to the brain, some of the million nerve fibres in each optic nerve cross over to the opposite side to give the sensation of depth perception. All the information goes to the visual cortex at the back of the brain and then to dozens of different areas of the brain, which process different parts of the image in different ways. Not even a supercomputer can match the brain's visual processing power.

History links

FOCUSING ON THE STARS

In 1604, in a publication about astronomy, the German scientist Johannes Kepler described for the first time how the eye focuses light.

Retina

In future, researchers hope to be able to give sight back to some blind people by implanting a light-sensitive chip in each retina.

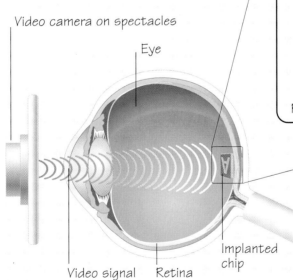

Video camera on spectacles

Eye

Video signal   Retina

Implanted chip

BIONIC EYES

A team of researchers at John Hopkins Hospital in Baltimore, Maryland, USA, is working on restoring sight to the blind. The researchers' ultimate goal is still many years in the future, but they have already succeeded in giving fleeting sensations of sight to patients who have been blind for up to 40 years. To do this they bypassed the light-sensitive rods and cones in the eyes and applied electrical signals directly to the nerves behind the retina. Depending on which nerves were stimulated, the patients saw spots of light, simple patterns and even letters of the alphabet. Increasing the number of electrodes enabled the patients to see more detail. The team is now constructing a system that will feed video images of the outside world to a chip fitted inside the retina.

CAMERAS

PHOTOGRAPHY HAS NEVER BEEN MORE POPULAR. PEOPLE LOVE TAKING PHOTOS SO MUCH THAT HUMANS ARE SNAPPING AWAY WITH ABOUT 800 MILLION CAMERAS WORLDWIDE. THERE ARE LOTS OF DIFFERENT TYPES OF CAMERAS, BUT THEY ALL WORK IN THE SAME WAY.

A camera works like a one-shot mechanical eye. A glass or plastic lens bends light before it passes through the aperture, a hole in the diaphragm. And that's as far as the light gets until someone presses the camera's shutter-release button to take a picture. Then, for a fraction of a second, the shutter opens and light is able to pass through and reach the film.

EXPOSURE CONTROL

The film has to be exposed to exactly the right amount of light to create a focused image. The camera controls this exposure in two ways. Changing the size of the aperture controls the amount of light entering the camera, while changing the shutter speed controls the length of time that light falls on to the film. The choice of shutter speed and aperture depends on what is being photographed. A fast shutter speed and a large aperture freeze moving objects, while a slower shutter speed and a smaller aperture capture slow or stationary objects in sharp detail. Automatic cameras select the shutter speed and aperture automatically.

Some cameras have a range of exposure control settings, varying from entirely automatic to entirely manual. In between, semi-automatic settings enable the photographer to set the shutter speed and the camera to select the aperture, and vice versa. There may also be automatic settings for different types of subject – for example, sports events, still subjects, portraits and shooting at night.

A camera fitted with a long lens produces enlarged images of distant objects.

TYPES OF CAMERAS

The two most popular types of cameras today are compacts and Single Lens Reflex (SLR) cameras. Compacts are smaller and lighter than SLRs. Both types can be controlled automatically by autofocus and exposure control systems, so they can be very easy to use. They differ in two main ways. Compact cameras are also called direct vision cameras, because you look through the viewfinder directly at the scene to be photographed. A separate lens focuses the image on to the film. An SLR uses the same lens to show the photographer the view through the viewfinder and also to expose the film. In addition, an SLR can be fitted with a range of different lenses – some for close-up shots, some for long-distance shots, and others to achieve special effects.

These cameras take photographs on standard photographic film, which has to be sent away to be processed. Instant picture cameras use a special type of film that develops into photographs before your very eyes. And digital cameras have no film at all. They record images electronically.

A compact camera (top) makes photography easy; a single lens reflex camera (bottom) gives the photographer more control.

History links

WATCH THE BIRDIE!

The first cameras were made in the 1830s. They were large, heavy wooden boxes and they used fragile glass plates. Early photographers carried these heavy cameras all over the world and brought back photographs of places that most people had never seen before. Photographic studios sprang up everywhere and everyone wanted to have their photograph taken. Early photographers had to take darkrooms and chemicals with them wherever they travelled, to process their glass plates. In the 1850s, photographers took horse-drawn darkrooms (right) with them to the Crimean War, the first major war to be photographed.

FILM

SOME MATERIALS ARE ABLE TO USE THE ENERGY IN LIGHT TO PRODUCE PHYSICAL OR CHEMICAL CHANGES – FOR EXAMPLE, GLASSES THAT DARKEN AUTOMATICALLY IN SUNSHINE. PHOTOGRAPHIC FILM REGISTERS MINUTE VARIATIONS IN LIGHT AND COLOUR AND RECORDS THEM PERMANENTLY.

When you take a photograph, light falls on to a piece of film behind the camera's shutter for perhaps less than one hundredth of a second. The energy in such a short burst of light is tiny, but it's enough to leave a lasting effect on the film. The light travels through three layers of chemicals called emulsions. Each emulsion is sensitive to one colour only. One responds to blue light, one to green and one to red. When light hits, silver compounds in each emulsion change to pure silver metal.

By the time the shutter snaps shut, one emulsion contains all the blue information in the picture, one contains the green information and one contains the red information. However, the film looks exactly as it did before you took the picture. The image it contains is invisible, so it has to be 'developed'.

The film is processed by dipping it in a bath of chemicals that change more of the silver compounds in the emulsions into silver metal. As the silver compounds change, they activate chemicals in the emulsions called couplers, which produce coloured dyes. A different dye forms in each emulsion, but they're not coloured blue, green and red – the light colours that originally hit the emulsions. Instead, the opposite or complementary colours are produced – yellow, magenta and cyan. These colours are chosen so that when light is shone through the 'negative' film on to a piece of 'positive' light-sensitive paper and the paper is developed chemically, the end-product – the photograph – contains the correct colours.

Top layer
Blue recording emulsion
Green recording emulsion
Red recording emulsion
Backing layer

A colour film is a complex stack of chemical layers (above). In the three light-sensitive emulsion layers, silver compounds are changed chemically when light strikes them.

INSTANT PICTURE FILM

Instant picture film has all the layers of colour of negative film plus several positive print layers and the processing chemicals. When you take a photograph with an instant picture camera, light streams through the transparent positive print surface and hits the light-sensitive layers. A motor pushes the film out of the camera between a pair of rollers. The rollers squeeze the layers of film and processing chemicals together. Within a minute or so, the chemicals have done their work and the photograph is fully developed.

Advanced Photo System (APS) cameras can take photographs in three shapes – classic (top), panoramic (middle) and HDTV (bottom).

ADVANCED PHOTO SYSTEM

The Advanced Photo System (APS) uses a new type of film. APS film is nearly one third thinner than other film because it is made from a plastic material called Poly-Ethylene Naphthalate. The film also has a transparent magnetic coating on the back that can carry a range of information for the photographer and processing laboratory. Photographs can be taken in three different formats. The extra-wide panorama format is good for landscape shots. The wide high definition (HDTV) format is the same shape as a widescreen television. The classic format is the traditional 35-millimetre frame shape.

History links

POTATO PRINTS

One of the first ways to produce colour photographs, the Autochrome process, depended on potatoes! The photographic plate was covered with millions of starch grains made from potatoes. The grains were dyed red, green and blue. The Autochrome process was invented in 1903 and it remained popular until the 1930s.

DIGITAL CAMERAS

THE LATEST CAMERAS WORK WITHOUT FILM! INSTEAD, THEY TAKE PICTURES ELECTRONICALLY AND STORE THEM AS COMPUTER DATA. THIS DATA CAN BE FED INTO AN ORDINARY PC, OR SENT ANYWHERE IN THE WORLD WITHIN SECONDS.

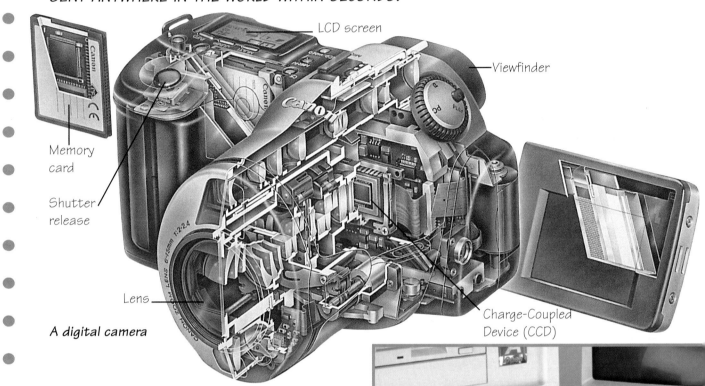

LCD screen

Viewfinder

Memory card

Shutter release

Lens

Charge-Coupled Device (CCD)

A digital camera

Instead of using film, a digital camera works like a video camera that takes still pictures. The pictures are stored on a chip or computer disc inside the camera. Because the pictures are saved electronically, they can be fed into a computer.

Once the pictures are in the computer's memory, they can be processed and manipulated by the computer like any other computer graphics. Digital photographs can be lightened, darkened, re-sized or edited. If part of an image is unsatisfactory, it can be changed, pixel by pixel. Then the pictures can be inserted into newsletters or other documents, or sent by email to another computer anywhere in the world.

Some digital cameras can be connected to a PC, so that they can download their photographs into the PC's memory.

Many newspaper photographers use digital cameras to send pictures to their newspapers by telephone. Only seconds after a picture is taken, it can appear on a computer screen thousands of kilometres away.

INSIDE A DIGITAL CAMERA

Light enters a digital camera through a lens, iris and shutter, just like a normal film camera. But instead of falling on to a piece of light-sensitive film, the light falls on a light-sensitive chip called a Charge-Coupled Device (CCD). Hundreds of thousands of separate light sensors in the CCD change the image into a pattern of electric charges, which are translated into digital data – numbers. This data is then stored in the camera's digital memory, or on a magnetic disk or memory card.

AS GOOD AS FILM?

The quality of a photograph depends on the numbers of spots of light, or pixels, that the picture contains. The least expensive digital cameras produce pictures composed of about 200,000 pixels each. That's about two thirds the quality of a typical computer screen. More expensive digital cameras produce sharper images, because the pictures are composed of more pixels. A resolution of 640 x 480 is equivalent to the picture quality of a typical PC. The most expensive digital cameras on general sale have a picture resolution of more than a million pixels. One boasts six million, but it costs more than most people pay for a car! The greater the number of pixels, the more finely detailed the picture.

Images transferred from a digital camera into a PC can be printed out in full colour, or incorporated in letters or other documents created by the computer.

Link-ups

INSTANT DIGITAL

Polaroid, the company that invented the instant picture camera, has developed a digital camera that produces an instant print. Most of the time, the camera works like a normal digital camera. But if the photographer wants a print, a pack of instant picture film is slotted into the camera which then prints out whatever is displayed on its liquid crystal display (LCD) screen.

ELECTRON CAMERAS

IT IS POSSIBLE TO MAKE PHOTOGRAPHS BY USING PARTICLES INSTEAD OF LIGHT. THE PHOTOGRAPHS PRODUCED ARE ACTUALLY MORE FINELY DETAILED THAN OPTICAL PHOTOGRAPHS. BUT THE CAMERA THAT PRODUCES THEM ISN'T USUALLY THOUGHT OF AS A CAMERA — IT'S AN ELECTRON MICROSCOPE.

Photographs taken by an electron microscope are called electron micrographs. These electron micrographs show a potato crisp (above) and human skin (right).

An electron microscope is an immensely powerful magnifying camera. It works by firing electrons at an object, analysing how the object affects the electrons and transforming that information into an image. Electrons are the tiny negatively charged particles that surround the nucleus at the centre of an atom. It may seem impossible to make a picture from particles instead of light, but the electron microscope relies on the fact that matter can change into energy and vice versa. Particles as small as electrons behave like particles some of the time and like electromagnetic waves at other times. So, electrons have wavelength, just like light or a radio wave.

An electron's wavelength is shorter than any light wave. The shortest light wave is about half of a thousandth of a millimetre long. Electrons used in electron microscopes have a wavelength that is roughly 5000 times shorter than this. As it is the wavelength that determines the size of the smallest detail in an image, electrons can produce much more finely detailed images than light.

THIN OR THICK?

There are two main types of electron microscope – the transmission electron microscope and the scanning electron microscope. A transmission electron microscope fires electrons through specimens, while a scanning electron microscope is used to bounce electrons off the surface of thicker specimens.

Inside a transmission electron microscope, a beam of electrons is fired down through an ultra-thin specimen less than 100,000th of a millimetre thick. Some of the electrons are absorbed or scattered by the specimen, but some pass straight through. The electrons that pass through are focused by electromagnetic lenses on to a fluorescent screen or a photographic plate.

Inside a scanning electron microscope, the electron beam scans back and forth across the specimen. When the electrons hit the specimen, they knock more electrons, called secondary electrons, out of the surface. The secondary electrons are collected and used to control the strength of an electron beam that produces an image of the specimen on a television screen.

Electron microscopes are used to do a huge range of jobs. In addition to scientific research, they analyse fibres, gunpowder deposits and other minute samples collected from crime scenes. They examine sooty deposits from inside jet engines to check on engine health and wear. And they are used to analyse a variety of biological samples – for example, the structure of individual cells and viruses.

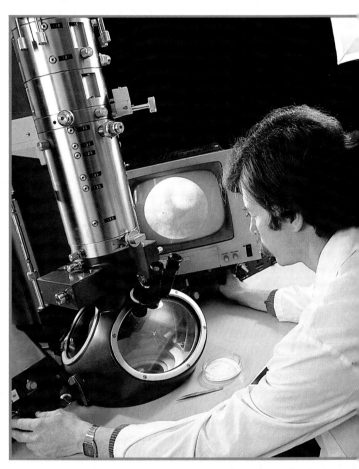

A scientist uses a transmission electron microscope to study magnified images of the virus responsible for causing influenza. The transmission electron microscope is 100 times more powerful than a light microscope.

SURFING THE MICROSCOPE NET

You don't have to be in the same room, or even the same country, as an electron microscope to use it! Some electron microscopes are linked to the Internet. It is possible to log on to the web site for one of these electron microscopes, control the microscope and receive images from it over the Internet. It enables experienced microscope users to supervise the work of less experienced users. It also allows several people in different places to log on to the web site at the same time and see the pictures from the same microscope.

History links

THE FIRST ELECTRON MICROSCOPE

In 1926, Hans Busch described how an electron microscope would work. Two years later, Max Knoll and Ernst Ruska started work on Busch's research. The result, in 1931, was the construction of the world's first electron microscope.

EYE SPY

CAMERAS ARE BEING MADE IN INCREASINGLY MINIATURE VERSIONS AND THEY CAN BE OPERATED FROM SOME DISTANCE AWAY BY REMOTE CONTROL. THEY ENABLE US TO SEE IMAGES AND TO LOOK AT EVENTS FROM VIEWPOINTS THAT WOULD OTHERWISE BE IMPOSSIBLE.

The development of miniature cameras and lenses means that we can now watch sports events from angles and from viewpoints that were impossible a few years ago. Miniature video cameras give us a driver's eye view of a Formula One motor race. The smallest cameras can be built into a cricket stump, to show the unnerving sight of the ball hurtling towards the batsman at knee level. Remote control cameras are also sometimes used to capture photographs in places where it is too dangerous for a photographer to be.

3-2-1-LIFT-OFF!

You may have seen close-up photographs of the Space Shuttle taking off, with jets of fire pouring from its engines. No one is allowed near the Space Shuttle during a launch, but photographers are taken out to the pad the day before a launch so that they can set up their remote cameras. These cameras and their remote-control equipment are powered by batteries. Space Shuttle launches are sometimes delayed and while the Shuttle remains fully fuelled, no one is allowed to approach the pad. So photographers just have to cross their fingers and hope that their batteries hold enough charge to

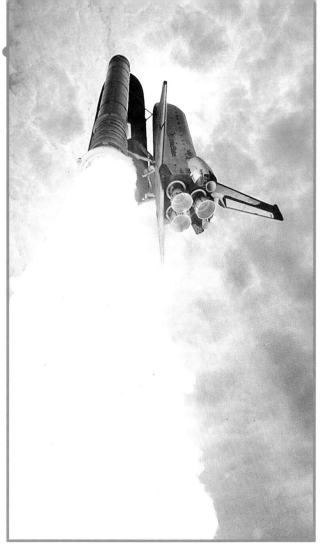

A remote camera captures a worm's eye view of the Space Shuttle soaring away into the sky from its launch pad.

power their equipment when the Shuttle's engines do, eventually, fire! When the Shuttle does take off, the remote cameras are triggered by radio signals or by the sound of the Shuttle's engines. The sound of a Space Shuttle taking off is incredible. Even five kilometres away the vibration, shock waves and noise make spectators feel as if their insides are being scrambled.

NIGHT SIGHTS

Modern photographic film can record images in remarkably poor lighting conditions. But there comes a time when there is not enough light for even the most sensitive film. One answer is to provide more light. If that is not possible, another solution is to use heat-sensitive, infrared film. If that isn't possible, another answer is to use an image intensifier. Even when it is so dark that the human eye can't see anything, there is still some light. An image intensifier changes the small amount of available light into electric currents, amplifies them electronically and then changes them back into light again. The brighter image produced by the image intensifier is light enough to be photographed or filmed.

DRIVER BEWARE!

Motorways and road junctions are often monitored by video cameras that spot traffic jams and accidents. Dangerous roads and junctions are sometimes also monitored by a different type of camera – a still camera. This type of camera is triggered by a vehicle's excessive speed and photographs its number plate. The mere sight of a camera can deter drivers from exceeding the speed limit.

An ingenious type of camera has been used to photograph accidents at road junctions, to analyse why they happen. This camera records images electronically every fraction of a second. But the images are erased unless the camera's control system detects the distinctive sound of a car crash. Then, the images just before, during and after the crash are saved for analysis.

Different types of camera are used to measure a car's speed (below) and to record road accidents (right).

History links

NIGHT EYES

Image intensifiers have been developed for military use. They enable tank crews to find the enemy, and helicopter pilots to keep flying safely after dark. They have become so compact and portable that individual soldiers fit night sights to their rifles. Military image intensifiers can boost the brightness of a view up to 40,000 times.

Link-ups

REMOTE CONTROL

Remote control cameras can be triggered by a range of remotely operated shutter releases. They can be fired manually by the photographer, using a remote control handset. They can also be fired automatically by a switch that is triggered by sound, light, heat, a motion sensor, or by a touch-sensitive wire or pad.

FALSE COLOURS

THE MANUFACTURERS OF FILM, CAMERAS, LENSES AND TELEVISION SCREENS NORMALLY TRY TO ENSURE THAT THE COLOURS SHOWN IN PHOTOGRAPHS AND ON SCREENS ARE AS CLOSE TO REALITY AS POSSIBLE. BUT SOMETIMES IMAGES ARE DELIBERATELY GIVEN FALSE COLOURS.

There is an old saying that a picture is worth a thousand words. It's another way of saying that humans can take in visual or pictorial information and understand it much more easily than pages of words or numbers. Before the computer age, changing information from text or numbers into pictures was extremely time-consuming because of the huge amounts of calculations that had to be made. Of course, computers are very good at doing large calculations very quickly, so it's now easier than ever to produce information in visual form.

When a new part is designed for a vehicle, it is often simulated on a computer screen. The simulation checks that the part fits and does its job properly.

PICTURING THE INVISIBLE

The human eyes and brain interpret different wavelengths of light as different colours, but we cannot see the waves that are beyond the red and violet ends of the rainbow spectrum. One way of making these invisible waves visible is to give each wavelength or group of wavelengths a different colour to make a false-colour image. It's like shifting the inaudible squeaks of a bat or a dolphin down in pitch so that human beings can hear them.

A false-colour image is much easier to understand than columns of numbers representing the intensity of different wavelengths at different points. But the false colours need not mean intensity or brightness. They can be used to label different temperatures, pressures, speeds, heights, types of rocks or vegetation. Almost any type of information can be coded using colours in this way.

COMPUTER SIMULATIONS

When new aircraft, cars, ships, rockets or spacecraft are being developed, the designs are often checked by using computer simulations. A computer can show how the air pressure changes as the air flows around the vehicle and how a vehicle is heated by the air rubbing against it as it travels at high speed. Thermal images of everything from soup cans to parts of jet engines are colour-coded using a similar method.

In this false-colour satellite image of Denver, Colorado, USA, healthy plants appear red, bare soil is green and built-up areas are light blue.

Link-ups

HAND COLOURING

The earliest movies were made with black and white film. One controversial use of false colour is to add colour to these old movies (for example, Laurel and Hardy, left). Tens of thousands of frames have to be coloured individually. This used to be done by hand with a paintbrush, but now computers do a lot of the routine colouring. Adding colour to a black and white movie is called colourisation.

History links

FALSE FALSE COLOURS!

When the Viking space probes landed on Mars in 1976, the first photos from the surface of the planet showed a pink sky. Mission controllers on Earth thought that this couldn't be right and so they altered the colour balance of the pictures so that the sky was blue. Later, one of the cameras was pointed at a colour reference card fixed to the space probe, but the colours were all wrong. When they were corrected, the sky was indeed pink!

CAMERAS IN THE SKY

Remote-sensing satellites carry detectors that are sensitive to infrared energy as well as light. Built-up areas, and different types of vegetation, rocks, ice and water all reflect wavelengths of light and heat in different ways. By photographing the ground at different wavelengths, satellites can easily pick out features of plants, crops, rocks and minerals that may not be easily visible on the ground. Oil companies use satellite photographs to look for rock formations where oil might be found. Government agencies and environmental organisations use them to monitor pollution. Planning authorities use them to study the different ways in which land is used – for building, agriculture and roads – and how it might be used in future. Forest managers use them to map forests and identify the distribution of different species of trees.

MOVING PICTURES

CINEMA FILMS ARE A MAJOR GLOBAL COMMUNICATIONS MEDIUM. HOLLYWOOD MOVIES HAVE SUCCESSFULLY SPREAD AMERICAN CULTURE ALL AROUND THE WORLD. EVER SINCE THE EARLIEST DAYS OF THE MOVIE INDUSTRY, FILM-MAKERS HAVE USED THE LATEST TECHNOLOGICAL TRICKS TO CREATE AMAZING IMAGES AND SOUNDS.

Almost any image a director wants can be created by computer for the screen. *Jurassic Park* stunned cinema audiences with its computer-generated dinosaurs. Now computers have finally mastered the most difficult effect – natural, realistic human movement. Two films in particular – *Toy Story*, made in 1996, and *Titanic*, made in 1997 – have demonstrated the possibilities of imaging technology in the movies.

Computer generation brought dinosaurs to life in Jurassic Park (above) and created characters such as Mr Potato Head in Toy Story *(right).*

TOY STORY

The movie *Toy Story* broke new ground in computerised movie imaging. There were no sets, no cameras, no film and no actors. The entire film and all of its colourful characters were created by computer. The story came first. It was sketched out, scene by scene, to form a storyboard. Then a full-length version of the film was made, with a stationary sketch standing in for each scene. All the scenes were assigned to computer animators.

Each animator started with a simple stick figure and moved it through a scene to ensure that the actions worked. Then the stick figure was given a 3-D body shape with realistic textures and colouring. Finally, lighting was added, so that the highlights and shadows fell in the right places. The images were then sent to a machine called a film setter, which used lasers to draw them, one by one, directly on to the film. Over 110,000 frames of film were created individually in this way. In all, *Toy Story* took 800,000 hours of computer time to complete.

TITANIC

As the camera rears up into the air and the massive hull of the *Titanic* slips beneath it, dozens of people walk about on the deck of the giant liner. It might have been shot from a helicopter, but it wasn't. There was no ship and the people who appear to walk about were not live actors. The ship was a 1/20th scale model photographed on a film set, and all of the passengers strolling about its decks were computer-generated. *Titanic* was directed by James Cameron. He also made the *Terminator* movies, which pushed computerised imaging to the limits of the technology.

VIRTUAL CINEMAS

The audience of a 21st-century movie settles back and begins to watch the film. But there is no screen at the front of the theatre. Some of the film-goers are watching a science-fiction movie while others are watching a horror feature. Some are listening to a soundtrack in

History links

COMPUTERISED IMAGING

The Disney film *Tron*, made in 1982, was the first movie that mixed computer-generated images with live action. The five-minute film *Tin Toy*, made in 1993 at Pixar by John Lasseter, was the first film in which every frame was created entirely by computer.

English, while a group of French visitors hear the soundtrack in their own language. Each person in the audience wears a device called a virtual retinal display which beams movies directly on to the retina at the back of the eye. When the viewer puts on a headset, he or she chooses which film they want to watch and selects the soundtrack language.

Until the virtual retinal display is introduced, films will continue to be projected on to a screen. But there may be no film in the projection room. Ways of distributing films to cinemas by digital radio via satellites are being developed and tested. Films distributed digitally by satellite will be stored and projected electronically.

Link-ups

DIGITAL CLOTHING

Until now, computer animators have found it very difficult to make a digital character's clothes fold, stretch and move in a lifelike way. In the future, digital actors will be clothed more realistically, thanks to a new generation of animation software packages. These packages allow animators to choose different materials for different clothing. The various materials will then behave according to their real properties.

CHANGING GEAR

TIME TICKS ON INEXORABLY. THE PRESENT IS WITH US FOR AN INSTANT AND THEN IT SLIPS INTO THE PAST. SO FAR, WE HAVE NOT FOUND THE SECRET OF TIME TRAVEL, BUT PHOTOGRAPHY AND ELECTRONIC IMAGING ALLOW US TO SQUASH TIME OR STRETCH IT IN WAYS THAT ARE IMPOSSIBLE IN THE REAL WORLD.

Our eyes can separate events if they happen more slowly than about 30 times a second. Any faster than that and movements merge together in a blur. However, film cameras and electronic cameras can record images much more quickly than the human eye. By filming something with a high-speed camera and then playing the film back at slower speed, time is stretched and movements that are a blur to the human eye become clearer.

The wings of the smallest humming birds flap at up to 80 beats per second – far too fast for humans to see. High-speed film of a humming bird can slow down its wing movements so that we can see them clearly. The same technique is used by photo-finish cameras to separate athletes who appear to cross the finish line together at the end of a race.

The wing motion of a humming bird is revealed by high-speed photography.

QUICK, QUICK, SLOW

Scientists use high-speed filming to study fast events. A lightning strike between a thunder cloud and the ground looks like a single flash of light – one giant spark. But when it is slowed down by high-speed filming, the lightning strike is revealed to be much more complex. The first flash, the leader stroke, sets out from the cloud to the ground. Its negative electrical charge repels negative charges in the ground below, producing a strong positive charge on the ground. This produces a second flash from the ground up to the cloud – the return stroke. The leader and return strokes meet about 50 metres above the ground and short-

A photograph freezes a moment in time as a pair of lightning bolts flash from the base of a thundercloud to the ground.

Slow-motion filming reveals exactly what happens when a van hits a wall at 48kph. The dummies inside the van are designed to move in the same way as humans in a crash.

Link-ups

STOP MOTION ANIMATION

The technique of building up a film frame by frame is used to make animated films. A frame is photographed every few seconds. Between frames, the puppets and background are moved a fraction according to a detailed plan. When the film is shown at normal speed, all these tiny, fractional changes merge together to produce the illusion of smooth movement. This technique is called stop motion animation.

circuit the cloud to the ground, causing the brightest flash, which lasts only about 70 microseconds (millionths of a second). There may be several leader-return stroke events in a fraction of a second.

History links

SHUTTLE TRAGEDY

When the Challenger Space Shuttle broke up just after lift-off on 28 January 1986, slowed-down film of the launch revealed the cause of the tragedy. A seal between two sections of one of the solid rocket boosters had become hardened in the cold weather, allowing a jet of hot gas to escape. It scorched a hole in the external fuel tank and burned through a support linking the booster to the tank. The spacecraft broke up in a giant fireball.

High-speed filming is also used to check the way missiles fly, to analyse what happens during a car crash, to test airbags in cars, to show how parts of machines fail or break, to show very fast chemical reactions – and for many more applications.

At the other end of the speed scale, things can happen so slowly that the naked eye sees little or no movement. By filming slow events, such as a flower opening or the rise and fall of the tide, and showing the film at faster speed, slow events are speeded up and become clearer. Speeded-up film shows how clouds build and storm clouds form, how people behave in crowds, how fallen leaves or dead creatures rot away, how plants move to follow the Sun, how cells grow and divide, and many other fascinating processes.

LASER PICTURES

PHOTOGRAPHS ARE FLAT AND TWO-DIMENSIONAL, BUT THE REAL WORLD IS THREE-DIMENSIONAL. IMAGINE LOOKING INTO A PHOTOGRAPH THAT CHANGES AS YOU MOVE YOUR HEAD — JUST LIKE THE REAL WORLD. ONE TYPE OF IMAGE, THE HOLOGRAM, DOES PRECISELY THAT.

In the movie *Star Trek*, the holodeck allows its fictional astronauts to get some relief from their starship's monotonous interior by creating environments such as rainforests, deserts, cities and beaches. It achieves this by generating holograms. It's the ultimate in virtual reality.

THE 3-D EFFECT

A hologram is not an image. It is a pattern that interferes with light. When light passes through a hologram or reflects off it, the pattern changes the light, creating the illusion of having bounced off the actual objects that you see. It has reconstructed a part of the world that is not there any more. The first holograms were made with lasers and had to be viewed with a laser. Later, scientists learned how to make holograms that could be seen in ordinary daylight.

So far, people have used holograms as security seals on products ranging from credit cards and bank notes to pre-recorded video cassettes. Holograms are still so difficult to produce that even the multi-billion dollar trade in fake products hasn't mastered their manufacture yet. They are also exhibited in galleries as pieces of art.

Science-fiction writers and film-makers quickly became fascinated by holograms and lost no time in exploring their possibilities. When Princess Leia had

Holograms are printed on credit cards and other items to make it more difficult for criminals to forge them.

A visitor to a hologram museum in Paris admires some circular holograms.

problems in the movie *Star Wars*, she sent for help by making a holographic video message that was carried away by the robot R2D2. *Star Trek* solves its shortage of medical staff by generating a holographic medical officer when necessary. And Arnold Schwarzenegger foiled the baddies in *Total Recall* by generating multiple holographic images of himself to draw their fire.

3-D MOVIES

For more than 20 years, researchers have been working to try to produce moving holographic pictures. The major barrier to developing this technology is the huge amount of information that has to be processed every second. But real-time holographic imaging is now much closer to reality. In a future holo-cinema, the images will float in mid-air in front of the audience, looking more like actors on a live theatre stage than pictures on a flat screen.

Researchers at the Massachusetts Institute of Technology in the USA are working towards creating something like the *Star Trek* holodeck – and they think they can complete it within the next 20 years. They can already make holovideos, but they are tiny – 60mm high, 150mm wide and 150mm deep – and, at five frames per second, they are slow. Even this primitive holovideo system requires a room full of supercomputing equipment. Researchers are looking for the breakthrough that will allow them to produce a larger and faster video system, and at the same time shrink the control system. If they succeed, there could be some amazing arcade games on the way! And there are serious applications too – for example, in car design, architecture, education, and training systems for firefighters, pilots and surgeons.

History links

WAITING FOR LASERS

Holography, the science of making holograms, was invented as long ago as 1948 by the Hungarian-born scientist, Dennis Gabor (below, in a hologram). But holography was little more than a scientific oddity until lasers were developed in the 1960s. Lasers provided the intense light with all of its waves exactly in step with each other that was needed for practical holography.

Link-ups

HOLO-STORAGE

A hologram can be used to store masses of computer data instead of just one image. In theory, one small holographic cube could store all the information currently held in all the world's computers.

HEAT IMAGES

OUR EYES ARE SENSITIVE TO A VERY NARROW BAND OF WAVELENGTHS IN THE ELECTROMAGNETIC SPECTRUM. ANYTHING BEYOND THE VIOLET AND RED ENDS OF THE RAINBOW IS INVISIBLE TO US. BUT OTHER DETECTORS CAN PICK UP SOME OF THESE WAVELENGTHS AND USE THEM TO CREATE PICTURES. BEYOND THE RED END OF THE RAINBOW LIES INFRARED RADIATION — HEAT RAYS.

Thermal (heat) cameras and thermal images are used in industry, on the battlefield and by the police, firefighting and rescue services. People missing in a chaotic jumble of wreckage can sometimes be pinpointed by locating heat sources – the heat from their bodies. A thermal camera flown on a police helicopter can track criminals on foot or in a vehicle hundreds of metres below on the ground. Firefighters use helmet-mounted thermal cameras to see their fellow firefighters and the centre of the fire more easily in smoke-filled buildings. Thermal sights enable military helicopter pilots to keep flying safely at night. Troops on the ground use thermal vision aids to spot enemy movements after dark. In industry, thermal images can find faults and problems in products that are invisible to the naked eye.

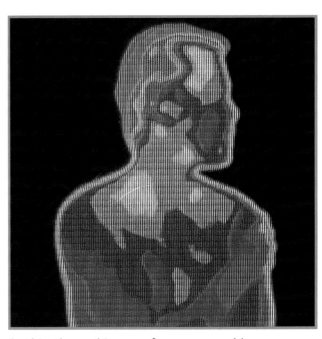

In this thermal image of a person, colder areas are shown in blue, while purple, orange and yellow indicate higher temperatures.

ON THE LINE

Many products are manufactured on high-speed production lines. In the canning industry, for example, dozens of cans may pass along the line every second. By the time a fault is spotted, hundreds of cans may have to be taken off the line and discarded. As cans are usually filled with hot liquids, a thermal imaging system can spot partly filled or leaking cans immediately, because the filled part of the can is hotter than the empty part. Even after a can is sealed, a thermal imaging system can still detect the liquid level inside it. By colour-coding the picture, the temperature of the can's contents can be checked visually to ensure that the contents have reached the right temperature to sterilise them.

Metal products, including cars, are often made by using a robot to weld the metal parts together. A thermal camera can check the welding work. It can show the temperature of each weld and also how far the heat has spread through the metal from the welding site. If parts near a weld have to be protected from heat, for example delicate electronics or plastic parts, a thermal camera can show how much or how little they have been heated and whether their safe limits have been exceeded.

Thermal cameras are also used to test and evaluate products. A car's brake system can be tested by looking at a thermal image of the system's brake disc. The disc heats up when the brakes are applied. A thermal image shows how evenly the disc heats, whether there are any hot spots that might weaken it or shorten its life, and how quickly it cools down again.

Pointing a thermal camera at the outside of a house or an office building shows clearly where heat is escaping from the building and where more insulation is necessary. A lot of heat escapes through windows. A building with a large glass area can have special 'low-emissivity' glass fitted instead of

In industry, thermal cameras are often used to check the quality of metal joints welded by robots.

ordinary window glass. A thermal image of this type of glass looks black because so little heat escapes through the glass.

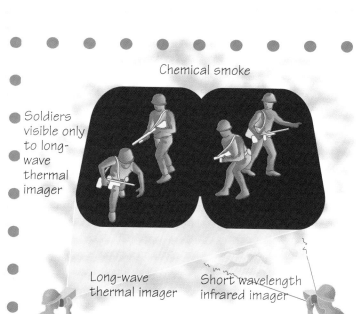

Chemical smoke

Soldiers visible only to long-wave thermal imager

Long-wave thermal imager

Short wavelength infrared imager

Scientists in the USA have developed a chemical smoke that obscures the battlefield to anyone without the correct imaging equipment.

Link-ups

STAYING ON TOP

Today, thermal imagers and artillery sights are used by almost every army, so the advantage they used to give to a few forces has vanished. US scientists are trying to give American troops the upper hand again by finding a way of blinding everyone else's thermal imagers while allowing their own to see clearly. They are developing a special chemical smoke which is opaque to thermal imagers that form images from short wavelength infrared rays, but transparent to longer wavelength infrared rays, so that only long-wave thermal imagers will see straight through it.

SPACE PHOTOGRAPHY

ASTRONOMERS AND SPACE SCIENTISTS CANNOT VISIT THE DISTANT STARS AND GALAXIES THAT THEY STUDY. BUT THEY CAN LEARN A GREAT DEAL ABOUT THESE FAR-AWAY OBJECTS BY ANALYSING THE ENERGY ARRIVING FROM THEM.

Photographs of the night sky are useful for plotting the positions of stars and galaxies, but the light that forms the photographs is only a small fraction of the energy sent out by stars. To some astronomers, light is the least interesting of all the energy emitted by stars. At first, scientists could only detect the presence or absence of different energies from certain spots in the sky, but as their instruments have improved, they have been able to make more detailed pictures.

RADIO PICTURES

The first of the new energies to be studied was radio. Scientists found that they could make pictures from the radio waves they received by giving the wavelengths different shades of grey or different colours. As a radio telescope scans across an object it takes reading after reading. Each reading is changed into a spot of grey or colour, building up a picture spot by spot, line by line, like a very slow television picture.

Astronomers discovered large radio outbursts of energy from objects, probably galaxies, so far away that they were too faint for optical telescopes to detect. They discovered giant jets of radio energy pouring out of some galaxies and they found stars that emitted regular radio bleeps as they spun. After radio, they looked for other wavelengths, but unfortunately most waves are absorbed as they pass through the Earth's atmosphere. So, this new branch of imaging and photography did not progress very far until the Space Age, when telescopes were first launched beyond the Earth's atmosphere and into space.

This map of the sky was created by the Compton Gamma Ray Observatory satellite. It shows gamma rays, not light. The band across the picture is our galaxy, the Milky Way.

This photograph, taken by the ROSAT satellite, shows X-ray emissions from a nearby galaxy, the Large Magellanic Cloud. The strongest emissions are shown in blue, while green, yellow and red are the weakest.

In this visible-light photograph of the constellation Orion, Betelgeuse is the bright star at the top of the picture. Betelgeuse is the strongest infrared source in the sky.

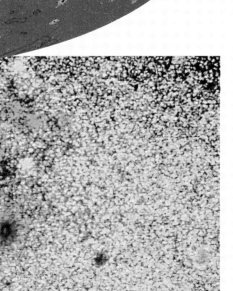

CUTTING THROUGH DUST

All objects give out infrared (heat) rays. The hotter the object, the shorter the wavelength of the rays. In an infrared photograph of the sky, blue stars are the dimmest, while red stars become the brightest. Infrared rays pass through the clouds of dust that normally hide distant stars from us, so infrared photographs show stars that are completely invisible to optical telescopes.

BEYOND THE VIOLET

A photograph of the sky at ultraviolet wavelengths looks very different from an optical or an infrared image. Only the hottest stars are visible. In the constellation of Orion, for example, Betelgeuse, a bright infrared source, disappears altogether in an ultraviolet photograph. But the three stars of Orion's belt shine brightly because they are very hot stars. Young stars are the hottest, so ultraviolet photographs show young, newly formed stars while cooler, older stars are invisible.

X-RAY TELESCOPES

Gas heated to more than a million degrees gives out X-rays. X-ray telescopes have detected places in the Milky Way galaxy where gas is heated to a scorching 100 million degrees. Gas rushing away from an exploded star, or supernova, is hot enough to emit X-rays. Astronomers think that X-rays are also given out when a small object, such as a black hole, sucks gas from a nearby star. As the gas atoms and molecules fall on to the black hole, they collide and rub together, heating up to enormously high temperatures. Scorpius X-1 is an X-ray source in the constellation Scorpio that may be caused by a black hole.

GAMMA RAYS

The most penetrating waves, gamma rays, are difficult to pick up and form into an image because they go straight through most detectors! One type of gamma ray telescope changes gamma rays into flashes of light. The faint light flashes are picked up by photomultipliers which amplify them and change them back into a brighter light – bright enough to form an image. Gamma rays come from the most violent events in the universe, including collisions between stars, exploding stars and collapsing stars.

BODY TALK

DOCTORS USE A RANGE OF DIFFERENT TYPES OF BODY SCANNERS TO LOOK AT IMAGES FROM INSIDE THE HUMAN BODY. SOUND, HEAT, RADIO WAVES, X-RAYS AND EVEN ANTI-MATTER PARTICLES ARE USED TO PROBE THE BODY AND FORM PICTURES OF ITS INNER WORKINGS.

The first hint that doctors might be able to see inside the human body without cutting it open came in 1895. The German-born Dutch scientist, Wilhelm Röntgen, noticed that a cathode ray tube was producing strange rays that could pass through everything except lead. He discovered that they passed through flesh, but were blocked by bones. Within a year, Röntgen's X-rays were being used in hospitals to make shadow pictures of patients' bones.

ULTRASOUND

Sonar has been used to detect submarines since 1917, by sending out pulses of ultrasound (very high frequency sound) and analysing the reflections that bounce back from objects. In the 1950s, doctors realised that an unborn baby is similar to a submerged submarine! Ultrasound soon replaced X-rays for scanning pregnant women. Since then, computers have greatly improved the clarity of ultrasound images.

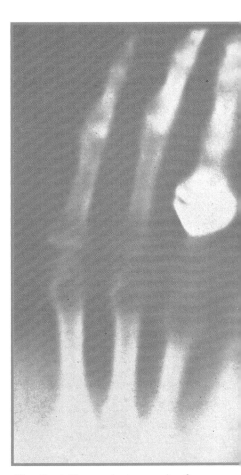

The first X-ray photograph of a human being was made in 1895.

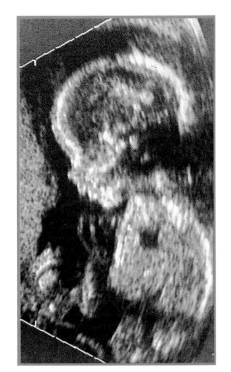

Unborn babies are routinely examined by giving their mothers ultrasound scans to make sure that the babies are developing normally.

SLICING UP BODIES!

In 1972, a new type of scanner was developed that combined computers and X-rays in a new way. It was called a Computerised Axial Tomography (CAT or CT) scanner. Beams of X-rays are fired at different angles through a patient. The ways the beams are affected by the body are analysed by computer and transformed into an image of a slice through the body.

Researchers at the Oak Ridge National Laboratory in Tennessee, USA, have developed a CAT scanner that can show details ten times smaller than other scanners.

They use it to study the effects of genetic mutations on the internal organs of small animals such as mice. Before the MicroCAT was developed, the animals had to be killed and dissected. Now, they can be studied in life.

NUCLEAR MEDICINE

While the CAT scanner was being developed, scientists elsewhere were working on an even more advanced scanner – the Nuclear Magnetic Resonance Imaging (NMR or MRI) scanner. The patient is placed inside a powerful magnet. Nuclei at the centre of some of the body's atoms line up with the magnetic field. Radio waves are directed at the patient and the lined-up nuclei absorb them. When the radio energy is turned off, the nuclei return to their normal state by releasing the radio energy again. The scanner receives and maps this radio energy. A computer then converts the radio signals into very detailed images of slices through the body.

LOOKING FOR ANTI-MATTER

The strangest scanner of all, the Positron Emission Tomography (PET) scanner, depends on particles of anti-matter called positrons. A positron is the opposite of an electron – the same size and mass as an electron, but with a positive electric charge instead of negative. A solution of weak radioactive glucose is injected into the patient. The radioactive glucose, which gives out positrons, enters the brain. The positrons collide with electrons and produce gamma rays. Sensors around the head detect the gamma rays and a computer uses them to construct an image of the brain. The brain takes up glucose when it is working, so a PET scan can show pictures of the brain in the act of thinking and processing information.

Link-ups

VITAL SIGNS
The University of Pennsylvania Medical Centre in Philadelphia, USA, is developing a new way of presenting information to doctors. This system shows an image instead of a series of separate numbers and levels. It takes the patient's heart rate, blood pressure, temperature and blood oxygen levels and combines them in a single 3-D chart.

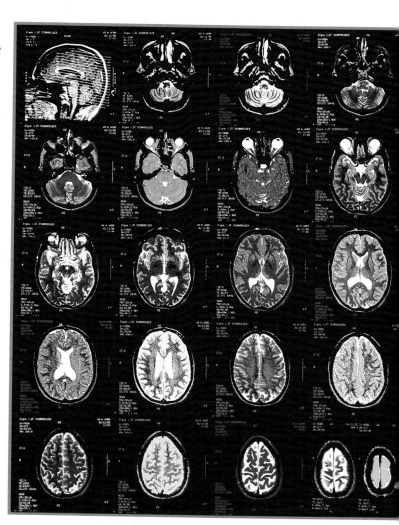

A Magnetic Resonance Imager (MRI) produces detailed images of the body's soft tissues, such as the brain, which do not show up well in X-rays.

FRACTALS

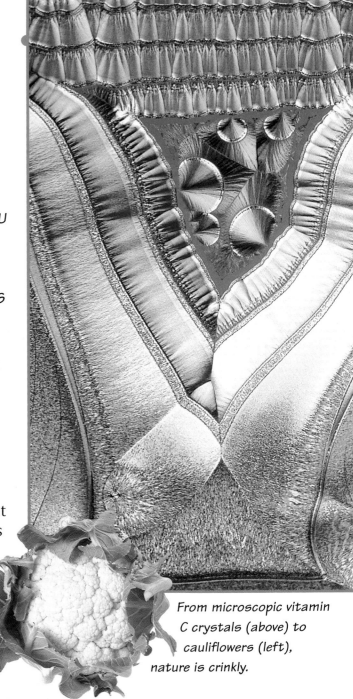

From microscopic vitamin
C crystals (above) to
cauliflowers (left),
nature is crinkly.

THE UNIVERSE IS CRINKLY! FROM COASTLINES TO TREE BARK, THE CLOSER YOU LOOK AT THE OUTLINES OR EDGES OF NATURAL PHENOMENA, THE SMALLER THE CRINKLES YOU SEE. WHEN MATHEMATICIANS FOUND EQUATIONS THAT PRODUCED THESE COMPLICATED ULTRA-CRINKLY SHAPES, IT TURNED OUT THAT THEY COULD BE APPLIED TO LOTS OF OTHER PROBLEMS INVOLVING HIGHLY COMPLEX INFORMATION, INCLUDING IMAGE-PROCESSING.

In the 1970s, mathematicians found that some of the crinkly, complicated shapes that are common in nature can be described and copied by very simple mathematical equations. The equations and the pretty patterns they produced were little more than attractive curiosities until mathematicians found that the reverse is true too – complex information can be broken down into simple patterns by using these same equations. This information provided solutions to practical problems such as how to store highly detailed images using the minimum of data, or how to send complex images over telephone lines that are incapable of carrying all the raw image data.

SHRINKING PICTURES

One of the problems involved in storing images electronically is that high-quality photographic images contain immense amounts of data. Because of this, storing and processing more than a handful of images is beyond the capabilities of the average home or office computer or CD-ROM drive. However, fractals offer a way of cutting down the data, so that images are much more manageable.

The key to the technique is that images, even highly complex images, can be broken down into a series of simple patterns. Instead of storing every single dot that makes up an image, the image is changed into a mosaic of these simple patterns, a bit like the pieces of a jigsaw. Then the computer stores the mathematical formulae that produce each piece of the pattern. This part of

The mathematical equations of Benoit Mandelbrot (see Link-ups box below) create beautiful and intricately detailed fractal patterns. The more closely you look, the more detail there is to be seen – just like the crinkly edges and surfaces found in nature.

Link-ups

THE MANDELBROT SET
The best known fractal patterns are generated by equations called the Mandelbrot Set, named after the mathematician, Benoit Mandelbrot. The word 'fractal' was invented by Benoit Mandelbrot from the Latin word *fractus*, meaning 'broken'.

the process can take a little time, but once the image has been analysed and coded in this way, it can be reconstructed very quickly. A digital code tells the computer which piece of the jigsaw to generate and display next, building up the picture piece by piece.

Aberdeen University in Scotland used fractals in this way to store a collection of 44,000 historic photographs. The photographs, on glass slides weighing five tonnes, were shrunk down on to a single CD-ROM! And, without fractals, Microsoft would have needed ten CD-ROMs to store all of the images on its *Encarta* encyclopedia. Fractals can reduce the amount of data needed to reconstruct an image to such an extent that it is even possible to send high-quality images over an ordinary telephone line.

BLOW-UP
You would think that an image produced from megabytes of original data would be much more finely detailed than an image generated from one hundredth the amount of data using fractals. But you would be wrong. Enlarge a standard image and the fine detail in it soon becomes jagged and coarse as the tiny pixels become enlarged. But blow up a fractal image and the enlarged image has even finer detail embedded in it. It is the fractal image that looks the more lifelike when enlarged, even though it was generated from less data. It seems impossible – but an enlarged fractal image is not simply a bigger version of the original. Each piece of the picture is generated by a mathematical formula. As the picture is enlarged, the mathematical formulae just keep on generating more and more detail.

IMAGES FOR ADS

PHOTOGRAPHS ARE USED TO SELL EVERYTHING FROM MAKE-UP, CLOTHES AND MEDICINES TO HOLIDAYS, CARS AND HOUSES. THEY PERSUADE US TO GIVE MONEY TO CHARITIES AND THEY ENCOURAGE US TO GO AND SEE THE LATEST FILMS.

Glamorous images such as this are widely used in advertising. Once the photograph has been taken, any imperfections can easily be removed on a computer to create a perfect picture.

Open any newspaper, magazine, brochure or catalogue and there are photographs everywhere. Advertising photographs show us products or services that we might buy. Sometimes, they show the product or service in a very straightforward way. Other advertising photographs encourage us to want a product or service by linking it to a lifestyle, or by creating a visual joke that makes us laugh and therefore makes us feel good about the product promoted in the advertisement.

Whatever the type of advertisement, the appearance of the photograph is vitally important. It has to be just right. If it isn't, then it has to be changed. Advertising photographs and magazine cover photographs are often altered by a process called retouching. Retouching used to be done by hand, using paint and paintbrush. But now, digital retouching has replaced the paints.

One of these pictures has been altered using a computer program. It's easy to spot the difference here, but advertisements often use very sophisticated techniques to enhance pictures.

DIGITAL RETOUCHING

A photograph with imperfections can be enhanced, or improved, by computer processing. The photograph is scanned into a computer. When it appears on the screen, parts of it can be enlarged and altered. The individual spots of brightness or colour in the picture, called pixels, can be changed one by one, or larger areas can be changed by a technique that copies the effect of a paintbrush or an airbrush. A bruise on an apple can be airbrushed out. The colour of the bruise is changed to match the rest of the apple. A spot on a model's face can be removed in the same way. Unwanted marks, reflections or shadows of any sort can be removed digitally. People can even be taken out of a photograph to concentrate the viewer's gaze on the really important part of the image. The glamour and appeal of a photo in a magazine today, especially a cover picture, may have as much to do with the skill of a computer operator as to the photographer's art. Filmed advertisements can be digitally processed, too, frame by frame.

CLIPS AND TAPE

Advertising photographs featuring beautiful models, men or women, look great. The models' hair and make-up are faultless and their clothes fit perfectly. Or do they? If you could look at the model from behind, you might find an odd collection of clips and tape holding the clothes in precisely the right way. Photographers spend an age setting up a 'shoot'. An unflattering crease or fold in clothing is not acceptable, so the clothes are pulled and tightened and fixed in place to get the best photograph possible. Even parts of the model's body may be 'altered' temporarily. Protruding ears may be stuck back against the head. Poses and lighting are arranged carefully to avoid unflattering shadows or creases in the skin. Only the most static sets can be photographed in this way. Other photographs require models to move around, dance, jump or walk. These are more natural photographs, with clothes flowing and folding naturally.

link-ups

SPACE ADS

Advertisements are shot either in studios or outdoors 'on location'. The most exotic and literally 'out of this world' location for an advertisement was the Russian Mir space station. Two advertisements have been filmed there. In 1996, Pepsi shot an advert for its new drinks can packaging. And, in 1997, the space station was the location for an advertisement for a brand of Israeli milk.

PHOTO DISCOVERIES

IMPORTANT DISCOVERIES HAVE BEEN MADE, AND ARE STILL BEING MADE, BY ANALYSING PHOTOGRAPHS. CAMERAS ACCOMPANY EXPLORERS TO THE BOTTOM OF THE SEA AND INTO SPACE. OCCASIONALLY, THEY REVEAL SURPRISES.

Photography has been around for more than a century, but it is still used by scientists and explorers to record events and make visual studies. And it still turns up interesting discoveries. Astronomers use photography and electronic imaging extensively. By comparing images of the same object or the same patch of sky taken on different nights, any changes can be spotted immediately. The planet Pluto was discovered by comparing photographs of the same patch of sky on successive nights and spotting that one of the 'stars' appeared to be moving differently from the others. This strange 'star' was Pluto. Today, photographs taken by the Hubble Space Telescope are giving astronomers new insights into the Universe and how it works.

BLACK SMOKERS

In the 1970s, scientists began to explore the ocean floor with deep-diving submersible craft – mini submarines. Some were manned craft, but many were unmanned camera platforms. The cameras had to be sealed inside special pods to protect them from the immense, crushing pressure of the surrounding water. Their photographs revealed some unexpected things.

This amazing photograph, taken by the Hubble Space Telescope, shows stars being formed in vast pillars of gas and dust in the Eagle Nebula.

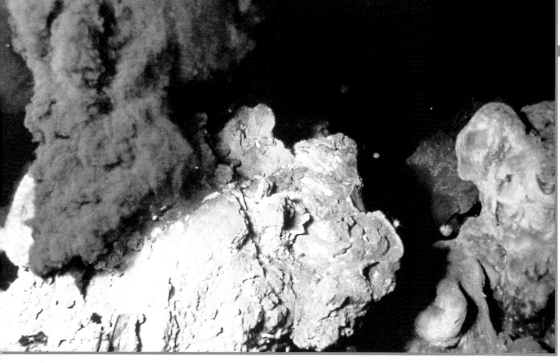

Hydrothermal vents, or 'black smokers', were photographed at the bottom of the Atlantic Ocean.

One of the most surprising was the hydrothermal vent, or 'black smoker'. These are rocky chimneys on the ocean floor which have dark, mineral-rich water billowing out of the top – hence their name. They are caused by volcanic activity beneath the ocean floor which heats up cold water seeping down through cracks in the rocks to more than 350°C. As the hot water spurts out through the surface rock again, the minerals in the water gradually build up a vent or chimney. Photographs showed that there were colonies of creatures, from bacteria to crustaceans and fish, living in these 'islands' of hot water, something that neither geologists nor biologists had anticipated.

THE SEARCH FOR THE *TITANIC*

Scientists in manned submersibles often stumble across shipwrecks on the sea bed. It occurred to some ocean explorers that mini submarines could be used to search for famous wrecks that had never been located because they lay in water too deep for divers to work in. One of these explorers, Dr Robert Ballard, set out to find the *Titanic*, the most famous wreck of all. The *Titanic* sank after hitting an iceberg in the north Atlantic Ocean in 1912. Ballard developed new deep-sea

imaging technology to help his search. Instead of shooting film which had to be brought to the surface and developed, he used camera technology borrowed from the television industry. This technology allowed him to view colour images from the mini submarine as they were being shot. He also used sonar to find large objects and a magnetometer to confirm that they were large metal objects. On the morning of 1 September 1985, Ballard finally found the *Titanic* lying in two pieces in nearly 4000 metres of water. The images captured by his cameras are breathtaking.

History links

CUBAN MISSILE CRISIS

In 1962, photographs taken by high-flying American U-2 spy planes revealed a Soviet missile launch site in Cuba, off the US coast, with more missiles bound for Cuba on the decks of Soviet ships. The United States blockaded Cuba, stopping all ships from reaching the island. Faced with the photographic evidence for all the world to see, the Soviet Union removed its missiles from Cuba. The USA also secretly agreed to remove missiles aimed at the Soviet Union from Turkey.

PROOF POSITIVE

THERE IS A WELL-KNOWN SAYING THAT 'THE CAMERA NEVER LIES'. ALTHOUGH CAMERAS MERELY RECORD THE IMAGE IN FRONT OF THEM, PHOTOGRAPHS CAN BE MISLEADING – BY DESIGN OR BY ACCIDENT. EVEN SO, PHOTOGRAPHIC EVIDENCE IS OFTEN ACCEPTED AS CONVINCING PROOF.

The police began using photographs to record the faces of convicted criminals in the 1840s, not long after photography was invented. Nowadays, police, fire and rescue services photograph and video the scenes of crimes, fires and rescue operations. Photography is still an important way of studying puzzling scientific mysteries.

DANCING SPRITES AND ELVES

There have been reports of strange lights streaming high in the sky above thunderstorms since the 19th century. People thought that they might have been reflections of lightning – or perhaps they didn't exist at all. Whatever they were, they remained a mystery until the 1980s, when they were seen in a video recording of a storm. Scientists went back through hundreds of hours of video recordings made from the Space Shuttle and found more of these streamers, called sprites. They then set out to photograph them from a high-flying NASA jet, using ultra-sensitive film. They succeeded in capturing 19 images. These images showed that the sprites were huge – 60 kilometres across, and shooting up 90 kilometres at a speed of 100 kilometres per second. Since then, scientists have photographed four different types of electrical activity in the upper atmosphere. Two, called sprites and elves, are now understood, but the other two, called blue jets and gamma ray events, remain a mystery.

PHOTOGRAPHIC ANALYSIS

The absence of a convincing photograph can lead people to believe that something doesn't exist. Despite thousands of sightings of strange animals and flying saucers, no one has taken a photograph that proves, once and for all, that these phenomena exist.

Photographs and films that are claimed to show strange creatures such as the Loch Ness Monster (above) and Bigfoot (right) have so far failed to convince everyone that these creatures exist.

Photo-reconnaissance, taking photographs of enemy territory, began during World War I and was used extensively during World War II. Photo-interpreters, the people who examined the photographs in minute detail, became experts in analysing photographs. Nowadays, in addition to their military work, photo-interpreters may be asked to examine photographs of objects ranging from the Loch Ness monster to Unidentified Flying Objects (UFOs).

It is important to discover whether or not these photographs are fakes. Does a photograph show a big cat, such as a puma, roaming the English countryside, or is the creature in the photograph just a large domestic cat? Does a photograph show a meteor skimming the Earth's atmosphere or is it ball lightning or an alien spacecraft? Photo-interpreters look at the direction and lengths of shadows, the amount of blurring and the sharpness of focus to find out if the distances, speeds, sizes, heights and viewpoint are as the photographer claims.

HOLLYWOOD'S LEGACY

The wonderful achievements of the creators of special effects in movies show that almost any image can be created on film. This means that photographs of monsters or aliens are probably less credible now than ever before.

On 2 July 1947 something crashed to Earth near Roswell, New Mexico. Some people believe that it was an alien spacecraft containing the bodies of several aliens, although the US government has always denied this. In recent years, a film showing surgeons carrying out a post-mortem examination of an alien from the Roswell flying saucer came to light. However, the ability of Hollywood special effects and make-up experts to create believable images of alien worlds and creatures means that the film can't be regarded as proof of the aliens' existence.

Link-ups

CLEANING UP BLURRED IMAGES

Films and photographs of strange creatures and flying saucers are often fuzzy or blurred. Computers can clean up images so that they can be seen more clearly. Thirty years ago, a film was shot in California, USA, showing what appears to be the legendary Bigfoot, a giant ape-man. At the end of 1998, the film was enhanced using the latest computer techniques and experts say the cleaned-up images show something that looks suspiciously like a zip around the creature's middle!

IN THE NEWS

WE ARE SO USED TO BEING ABLE TO SEE IMAGES FROM ANYWHERE ON EARTH – AND EVEN FROM SPACE – THAT OUR MEMORIES OF THE WORLD'S MOST IMPORTANT EVENTS OFTEN TAKE THE FORM OF THE PHOTOGRAPHS OR FILMS THAT RECORDED THEM.

Still cameras, film cameras and video cameras accompany scientists, explorers and news-gathering teams on their travels all over the world. Astronauts take cameras with them into space. Satellites and space probes carry cameras to the furthest reaches of the solar system. If it happens, someone or something with a camera won't be far away.

THE FORCES OF NATURE

Mount St Helens is a volcano in Washington State, USA. It had been dormant since 1857. When it erupted on 18 May 1980, cameras recorded a remarkable sequence of images that showed the mountain collapsing in seconds, causing avalanches of ash and stone and 20-kilometre high explosions of gas and ash. When the dust cleared, the top 550 metres of the mountain had disappeared!

CHANGING LIVES

In 1984, the people of Ethiopia were gripped by a terrible famine caused by years of drought, failed crops and war. Film of the starving people was shot by Kenyan photographer and cameraman Mohamed Amin, with a voice-over by BBC correspondent Michael Buerk. The 'Biblical scale' of the disaster, as Michael Buerk described it, shocked everyone who saw it. Pop singer Bob Geldof responded by bringing pop stars

An onlooker with a camera recorded the spectacular scene as Mount St Helens in Washington State, USA, blew apart in a volcanic eruption in May 1980.

together to make a record to raise money for the people of Ethiopia. The artists who made the record were known as Band Aid. Other Ethiopian charity records were made in other countries. Then, early in 1985, Geldof was instrumental in organising an event that brought together one of the world's biggest television audiences. It was a pop concert called Live Aid that lasted a whole day, 13 July, with artists performing on both sides of the Atlantic Ocean. To date, Live Aid has raised 100 million US dollars. And all this stemmed from the film shot by Mohamed Amin. Sadly, Mohamed Amin died in 1996, when the Ethiopian airliner in which he was travelling crashed into the sea off the Comoros Islands.

Bob Geldof visited Ethiopia and Sudan many times to see how the money raised by Live Aid was being used.

BREAKING RECORDS

When anyone attempts to break a record, cameras are there to record it. When sprinters dip towards the finish line at the end of an important race, broadcast cameras, still cameras and photo-finish cameras record the moment. In 1997, the Thrust SSC set the first supersonic land speed record. Cameras on the ground and in the air recorded extraordinary images showing shock waves fanning out and stirring up the surface of the Black Rock Desert for 50 metres on each side of the car, like a giant pair of wings.

History links

THE POWER OF FILM

In the 1930s, airships such as the *Hindenburg* carried passengers to and fro across the Atlantic Ocean in great luxury. On 6 May 1937, the giant *Hindenburg* was manoeuvring towards its mooring mast at Lakehurst, New Jersey, USA, when the hydrogen gas inside the airship caught fire. The massive ship crashed to the ground, burning fiercely. Of the 97 people on board, 36 were killed. A news film camera captured the whole event and the film went round the world. It signalled the end of the passenger-carrying airship.

History links

THE VIETNAM WAR

Wars have been photographed since the early days of photography in the 19th century, but the Vietnam War (1955-75) was the first war to be covered day after day in newspapers and magazines, and on television. News photographs and film of the fighting turned the American public against the war and caused mass protests all over Europe and North America. Public opposition, soaring costs and unacceptable casualties led to the United States' withdrawal from the conflict in 1975.

TIMELINE

FILM AND PHOTOGRAPHY DATES

WORLD DATES

1727 The German physicist Johann Schulze notices that silver nitrate turns black after it has been exposed to light.

1777 The Swedish chemist Carl Scheele studies the effect of light on paper treated with silver chloride.

1796 Edward Jenner carries out the first vaccination.

1800 Alessandro Volta invents the battery.

1802 Thomas Wedgwood, son of the famous potter Josiah Wedgwood, makes shadow images of objects and drawings on paper treated with silver nitrate.

Richard Trevithick invents the steam locomotive.

1826 Nicéphore Niépce takes the first photograph. His photographic plate is exposed for eight hours.

1835 Niépce's partner, Jacques Daguerre, invents a new way of making a photograph on a metal plate. William Fox Talbot succeeds in making a photographic negative on paper.

1839 William Fox Talbot uses his paper negative to make a positive photograph. Hippolyte Bayard invents a way of making photographic positives directly on paper.

1840 William Fox Talbot invents the Talbotype, better known as the Calotype, a way of making lots of photographs from one negative.

1848 Edmond Becquerel succeeds in making a colour photograph, but can't make it permanent.

1850 Adolf Mietke and Johannes Gaedicke invent flash powder to create a bright flash of light for taking photographs.

1851 Frederick Scott Archer makes materials sensitive to light by treating them with collodion (gun-cotton dissolved in ether).

The Great Exhibition opens at London's Crystal Palace.

1852 Henri Giffard invents the airship.

1859 Construction of the Suez Canal begins.

1869 Charles Cros and Louise Ducos du Hauron, working independently, discover the subtractive process, on which all modern colour photography is based.

1871 Richard Maddox describes the first way of making photographs with dry plates.

1879 American George Eastman invents a machine for making photographic dry plates.

1881 George Eastman and Henry Strong start a company that becomes famous worldwide as Kodak.

1885 Karl Benz builds the first petrol-engine motor car.

1888 Kodak starts selling the first simple-to-use camera.

1889 Henri Reichenback invents celluloid roll film for George Eastman.

1891 Gabriel Lippmann makes the first direct colour photographs.

1903 The Lumière brothers invent the autochrome process for making colour photographs by coating a photographic plate with potato starch dyed red, green and blue.

Orville Wright makes the first sustained powered flight.

1912 The passenger liner *Titanic* sinks in the Atlantic Ocean.

1914-18 World War I.

1925 Paul Vierkotter patents a glass bulb containing flash material.

FILM AND PHOTOGRAPHY DATES

WORLD DATES

1926 Robert Goddard launches the first liquid fuel rocket.

1927 Charles Lindbergh makes the first non-stop solo flight across the Atlantic Ocean.

1929 The first practical flash bulbs are made.

1930 The planet Pluto is discovered by Clyde Tombaugh.
Frank Whittle invents the jet engine.

1931 Harold Edgerton invents the electronic flashgun

1935 Two US musicians, Leopold Mannes and Leopold Godowsky invent Kodachrome slide film.

1936 The German company Agfa invents Agfacolor colour print film.

1937 The *Hindenburg* airship crashes to the ground.

1939-45 World War II.

1942 Kodak invents Kodacolor colour print film.

1945 The first autofocus system is invented in Germany by Dr Kaulmann.

1947 Edwin Land, founder of the Polaroid Corporation, invents the instant picture camera.
Charles 'Chuck' Yeager makes the first supersonic flight in the experimental rocket-plane, the Bell X-1.

1953 The structure of DNA is discovered by James Watson and Francis Crick.

1957 The world's first artificial satellite is launched by the Soviet Union.

1961 Cosmonaut Yuri Gagarin becomes the first person to orbit the Earth in Vostok 1.

1963 Edwin Land invents a colour print instant picture film that develops inside the camera in 60 seconds.

1967 Christiann Barnard performs the first heart transplant.

1969 Neil Armstrong becomes the first human being to walk on the Moon.

1970 Garrett Brown invents the Steady Cam, a portable movie camera.

1971 The first Intel microprocessor is introduced.

1972 Edwin Land invents colour print instant picture film that develops by itself outside the camera.

1973 The Skylab space station is launched.

1976 The first compact autofocus camera is introduced by Konica.

1978 The first test tube baby, Louise Brown, is born.

1981 Sony develops the Mavica, the first filmless camera – it takes photographs electronically and saves them on a magnetic disc.

1981 The US Space Shuttle is launched for the first time.

1983 Kodak invents T-grain emulsion making film more sensitive to light.
Kodak invents Ektachrome, a very sensitive colour reversal film.

1984 Canon introduces its Still Video System D413 – a camera capable of taking colour photographs electronically, saving them on a magnetic disc and sending them along a telephone line.

1984 Kodak introduces DX coding, allowing a camera to detect the speed of a film automatically.

1986 Fuji invents the disposable camera.
The Mir space station is launched.

1990 Nelson Mandela is released from prison in South Africa.

1997 Andy Green sets the first supersonic land speed record in Thrust SSC.

GLOSSARY

APERTURE The hole in a diaphragm through which light travels to enter a camera. Some cameras have a fixed aperture, while others can be changed by the photographer.

ADVANCED PHOTO SYSTEM (APS) A type of film that is easier to load and use than standard film. It carries magnetically stored information that can be read by the camera and by the film-processing machine.

AUTOFOCUS A system that enables a camera lens to adjust itself automatically so that it forms a sharp image on the film.

AUTOMATIC EXPOSURE A system that enables a camera to set its shutter speed and aperture automatically, to allow precisely the right amount of light into the camera.

COMPACT CAMERA A type of small, easy-to-use camera.

COMPOUND LENS A lens that is itself made from two or more lenses, called lens elements, fixed together.

CONJUNCTIVA The transparent protective covering over the cornea at the front of the eye.

CORNEA The transparent 'skin' at the front of the eye, covered by the transparent conjunctiva.

DIAPHRAGM A set of overlapping blades inside a camera or a lens that can close or open to control the amount of light passing through.

DIGITAL CAMERA A type of camera that records pictures electronically instead of on film.

ELECTRON MICROSCOPE A microscope that forms images by using electrons instead of light.

EMULSION A light-sensitive layer on photographic film.

EXPOSURE The amount of light that falls on to the film inside a camera, controlled by the aperture and shutter speed.

F NUMBER A number that shows the size of the aperture in a camera's diaphragm. The bigger the number, the smaller the aperture.

FILM SPEED A number that shows how sensitive film is to light. The bigger the number, the more sensitive it is and the less light it needs to capture an image. ISO400 film is twice as sensitive to light as ISO200 film (ISO stands for International Standards Organisation).

FOCAL LENGTH The distance between a lens focused on something a great distance away and the point where a sharp image is formed.

FOCUS To move a lens closer to or further away from the film to form a sharp image.

FRACTAL A complex shape or pattern produced by a simple mathematical equation that repeats itself over and over again.

GAMMA RAYS Invisible electromagnetic waves shorter than 100-millionth of a millimetre long.

HOLOGRAM A flat image, produced by using lasers, that shows a three-dimensional view.

HOLOGRAPHY The production and use of holograms.

INFRARED Invisible electromagnetic waves from a thousandth of a millimetre to a millimetre long, between the red end of the rainbow and radio waves.

INSTANT PICTURE CAMERA A type of camera that produces processed photographs within a minute or so of taking the picture.

IRIS A ring of muscle inside the eye that opens or closes to control the amount of light entering the eye.

LATENT IMAGE The invisible image formed on a film inside a camera before it is processed.

LENS A curved piece of glass or plastic used to bend light rays and form a focused image inside a camera. The eye contains a natural lens.

LIQUID CRYSTAL DISPLAY (LCD) A small screen made from two sheets of glass with a special liquid in-between. Passing an electric current through the liquid changes the way that light travels through it. Different shapes are formed by allowing light to pass through some parts of the display but not others.

MULTIPLE EXPOSURE Opening a camera's shutter more than once without winding the film on in-between shots.

NEGATIVE An image on film or paper in which the light and dark areas and colours are reversed.

PANCHROMATIC FILM Photographic film that is sensitive to all colours.

PHOTO-RECONNAISSANCE Taking photographs of the ground from an aircraft or satellite to learn about an enemy's troop positions and weapons placements and the effectiveness of bomb and missile attacks.

PIXEL Short for 'picture element', one of the millions of tiny dots that, together, make up a picture on a television or computer screen.

RADIO Invisible electromagnetic waves, from one millimetre to thousands of metres long, beyond the red and infrared end of the rainbow spectrum.

RED EYE An effect seen sometimes in photographs taken with flash, when the bright flash reflects off the back of the eye and produces red pupils.

RETINA The light-sensitive membrane at the back of the eye.

REVERSAL FILM Photographic film that is used to make slides, also called transparencies.

SHUTTER A screen that covers the film inside a camera. It prevents light reaching the film until it is opened by the shutter release, when a photograph is taken.

SHUTTER RELEASE The button on a camera that is pressed to open, or release, the shutter and take a photograph.

SHUTTER SPEED A number that shows how long a camera's shutter stays open when the shutter release is pressed to take a photograph. A shutter speed of 1/30th of a second might be used to photograph a stationary object, while 1/1000th of a second might be needed to photograph a sharp image of a moving object.

SLIDE A frame of film with a positive image on it that is viewed by shining light through it. Slides are also called transparencies.

SLR (SINGLE LENS REFLEX) A type of camera in which the photographer aims the camera and composes the image through the same lens that will create the image on the film. A movable mirror enables the same lens to do both jobs.

THERMAL Involving heat. Thermal energy is heat energy.

THERMAL CAMERA A camera designed to make pictures from heat instead of light. As heat has no colour, false colours are added to the picture so that different temperatures stand out clearly from each other. A thermal imager produces thermal images on a screen.

VIEWFINDER The part of a camera that the photographer looks through to aim the camera.

X-RAYS Invisible electromagnetic energy, with waves between a 100-millionth of a millimetre and a millionth of a millimetre long. X-rays can pass through many types of matter.

INDEX

Internet link

You can find out more about some of the subjects in this book by looking at the following web sites:

http://www.nmpft.org.uk
(National Museum of Photography, Film & Television Bradford, UK)

http://www.agfaphoto.com
(Agfa film and photography web site)

http://www.klt.co.jp/Nikon/LAIRD
(Nikon thermal cameras)

http://www.hmt.com/hbwww0/hbfaq.html
(Frequently asked questions about holograms)

http://www.imax.com
(IMAX large format film system)

http://www.dolby.com
(Dolby Laboratories, inventor of the sound system used for most major movie soundtracks)

http://www.oscars.org
(US Academy of Motion Picture Arts & Sciences film awards)

http://www.kodak.com
(Kodak film and camera manufacturer)

http://www.minolta.com
(Minolta camera manufacturer)

http://www.canon.com
(Canon camera manufacturer)

http://wwwpolaroid.com
(Polaroid instant picture camera inventor)

http://wwwpixar.com
(Pixar Animation Studios)